The 20's Chronicles

A Guide on How to Successfully Navigate Through Family, Friendships, Show Business & Love

Bianca Bee

Copyright © 2016 Bianca Bee

All rights reserved.

ISBN: 1523316934
ISBN-13: 978-1523316939

Dedication

I would like to dedicate this book to all my Busyy Bees worldwide, who are constantly trying to find their way, and stay positive and focused through their journey to success.

Contents

	Acknowledgments	i
	Prologue	1
	About Me	3
	What You Will Learn in This Book	5
1	Family	10
2	Friendships	18
3	Internships & the Entertainment Business	25
4	Branding & Networking	35
5	Relationships & Self-esteem	51
	My Final Words	63

Acknowledgements

Thanks to all my family and friends for giving me the courage, wisdom, struggles, tears and drive to write my very first book.

Thanks to The Bianca Bee Show crew; I would not have gotten this far without you all.

Special thanks to my Busyy Bees for always believing in me and supporting me through this journey.

Last but not least, thank you to the people who motivated me to write my book series.

I mention names at the end of this book, so don't kill me if I left you out.

Love you guys!

I hope you guys are ready for this journey of finding my way through *The 20's Chronicles*.

Prologue

Being in your twenties is not easy. You are constantly battling between the real world, your dreams, your love life, and social life and last but not least yourself. Questioning what to do with your career, your parents telling you to get a job, getting a degree and not actually using it. The real world is dangerous at times. You don't know whom to trust, you don't know who you truly are yet, and every day you are learning something new.

In this book, you will get a peek into the 20's Chronicles of **relationships, friendships, career, family and entertainment.**

This book was inspired by me just sitting in class one day redoing my website and creating a lifestyle blog that helped me gain a lot of social media following. A woman named Monique reached out to me in regards to interviewing me about my show for a popular magazine. We did an over-the-phone interview, and she and I instantly vibed and talked on the phone for about two hours.

She was like, "So when are you turning *The 20's Chronicles* into a book?"

"What?" I replied. "Never! I am not an author."

"Yes, you are. Your articles are great. You should really think about it."

Four months had passed, and I totally didn't think about writing a book. Eventually, I had to take creative writing for my last year of college. I absolutely loved the teacher because she made us write consistently. I decided to begin writing my book. My teacher one day pulled me aside and said, "Your writing is great. Since you want to bee the next Oprah, I have a list of books I think you should read to help you gain more knowledge." I really loved her for that because I could tell she was very sincere and saw an amazing bright future for me.

A few months later, I spoke with a friend of mine, an author named Natalie. At the time we were just talking about life and entertainment and then she was like, "So, when are you writing your book?" It was just another confirmation to just go for it.

I didn't think this blog would eventually turn into a book. It was just me simply being myself and speaking real topics that I've either experienced or have seen growing up. I'm not perfect, but I can only tell you what I am growing to bee as I venture into the 20's Chronicles.

And FYI I am going to use the word "bee" as "be" through this book because I call myself Bianca Bee.

About Me

From a single parent home to bullying, to living out my dreams, to interning for the biggest corporations, to guys leaving me for other girls, to being in a big city alone, to having my own businesses and only just turning 21 during the time of writing my book...my journey has not been easy.

Growing up, I didn't have it all. I am from Detroit, Michigan, and lived in an environment of the streets. The first battle I had to deal with was seeing my parents divorce and also getting bullied at school at the same time. I didn't know how to balance those two things only being nine years old at the time. My mother got it together in a year, and we had our own place a year later.

The ventures of independence grew in me at a young age. I had to mature very quickly, and a lot of adults around me including family didn't understand why I was so mature. Adults would always say, "Bianca is going to be fast when she gets older."

I didn't understand why people always commented on me and how I carried myself. My mom just always kept it real with me, and I will always love her for that. I learned that if you want it, get it on your own. Independence has been around me since I was ten years old. That's all I knew as I matured into an adult, but that has been a beauty and curse.

Bianca Bee

The beauty is that I don't need anybody, but the curse is I do need somebody. I want to feel loved, I want my relationships to work, but in the past, they have tended not to work. However, we will get to that later on in this book.

What You Will Learn in This Book

I went through many stages while writing this book. It took over a year to mentally examine my life as a 20-something. I know people think, *Well, she's so young. What can we possibly learn from her?* And my response to critics is, "Even though I'm young, I've seen a lot, experienced a lot and have accomplished a lot." I'm a woman beyond my years.

In this book, you will learn a lot that will honestly shock you. I am going to elaborate on every experience, heart break, pain and success I have ever experienced or seen. I have broken down every section of the book below.

Families have their ups and their downs; however, you have to learn how to accept each other and love each other unconditionally even if it's from **loving them from a distance,** which we will talk about later in this book. I have so much gratitude for my family now that I'm an adult. Three people besides my parents whom I truly appreciate in my life are my aunt Renee, my second father Daryl and my grandma Shortie. They have supported me a lot through my journey as a woman, and I appreciate them for always having my back through my life in Los Angeles. In this section I'm going to teach you how to truly forgive people in your family who have hurt you. I also will open up about my relationship with my brothers and sister.

Friendships began when I hit high school. I was around older girls whom I went to dance school with. My friendships with these girls eventually made us start our own dance crew called Adamasity. I was 14 at the time and just loved dancing and being around them. We created a business and a sister pack with each other. However, friendships and business sometimes don't mix. I'm glad that was something I learned at a young age. People change, you grow apart, and you just don't mesh well with people like how you thought. We had attitudes, we were stuck up, and people in the city didn't like us. Having a bad attitude is not cute when you are a pretty girl because that's what people expect. Which is another thing I learned growing up. As we all split and parted ways, I discovered that you are who you hang around. In this section of the book, you will learn that you will outgrow friendships and that's okay.

Business is something I learned when I turned 16. I decided to start my own blog. The blog was called Harm0nie, and it was based on celebrity gossip, upcoming independent artists and the latest trends. I took blogging very seriously while in high school; it was like a job even though I wasn't getting paid for it. I enjoyed it. I loved it. I was gaining popularity by blogging, which was how I created The Bianca Bee Show, my non-profit organization and more. I realized that I was destined for LA. My mother had taught me to never work a job you don't like, which is why I have a lot of work and internship experience, which we will talk about later. I will teach you how to gain more knowledge and how to bee confident in your brand.

Los Angeles came my way when I turned 17. I left off for college, which was one of the most amazing beginning stages of my life as a young woman. I had to leave my mommy. I didn't have her anymore, which was difficult because I am her only child. However, I knew it would bee the best decision for me. She was happy for me living out my dreams. When I moved to LA, I was lonely, but I would lie to people and say I was happy. I didn't like the people. I didn't understand the criticism. I had to grow some balls in this city, or I was going to bee crushed. Once I changed my negative thoughts into positive ones and learned how to play this game, my journey to success began. I will share the ins and out of Hollywood, if you decide to move here.

Show Business began when I turned 19. I was two years into LA, and I was like, let me start my own clothing brand. I started it and realized it wasn't for me. I wasn't fully skilled at designing and knew that wasn't my passion. I then began **The Bianca Bee Show,** which would eventually become my dream and my journey to even more success. I talked to my old roommate Keyanah at the time and another film student Jessica who became the director of my show. We talked about what it would bee about and how we were going to make this happen. Those two ladies trusted me and believed in me, and I will always love them for that. Within just a month, I had a full lavish set, a full crew and was ready for the journey of Bianca Bee and The Bianca Bee Show. The show was based on beauty, entertainment and everything in between. I was interviewing celebrities and upcoming young entrepreneurs. Throughout this journey, I created a brand that became more than what I expected. I couldn't handle all of it at first. Being a businesswoman and only 19 at that, I didn't know I would lose people from my circle, lose some people from my crew, cry, bee broke and all of that. It was new to me. But I knew this was what I was made to do, and I would not give up. I still continue my show until this day, and The Bianca Bee brand is becoming something special. While still doing the show, I have a created a non-profit organization, a successful blog called The 20's Chronicles, and have ventured off into being a brand ambassador for companies all while being in school and working a part-time job.

Internships were the main reason I became a little bit wiser in business. I realized what I do and do not want as an entrepreneur in the future. In 2013, I decided to take the whole year off of working a part-time job and just do internships. My first internship was with a smaller production company; I was their social media intern. There, I met one of my amazing mentors, Roger. My next internship was with After Dark Films as a general intern. While there, I learned about promotions of new movies. My next internship was for Paramount Pictures, where I covered a huge event as an intern. At this internship I learned all about new gadgets in film, and networking kicked in. After that internship, I interned with Dark Child Record Company with famous songwriter and producer Rodney J. I learned about the music industry and A&R work. The next year I applied for an internship with The Oprah Winfrey Network and got it as a Deliverables Intern. My last internship in college was with TMZ, where I learned so much as a writer and how social media truly works. In this book, I am going to share with you the ins and outs of how internships work.

Relationships weren't the strongest in my life. I had all these great things going on; however, I still had no boyfriend. LA had taught me to bee heartless. I didn't believe in love. I didn't want to bee with anyone controlling because I didn't want a relationship like the people around me growing up. I wanted to bee "independent" and live my life. Guys my age didn't like me, so I've always dated older. However, dating older guys didn't always make me happy. It wasn't fun. I felt like I had to bee grown all the time. It would make me so mad that I would always get hit on by older guys and not guys my age. Relationships weren't and still aren't my specialty. Guys would leave me for other girls or play me, which made me play them back. That's why I never opened up or gave just one guy my attention because when I would like

The 20's Chronicles

somebody, it would all go downhill. I'm now finding myself and realizing my standards as a young woman, and that's all that matters. I will share about not only my dating experience and advice but also my on and off relationship of three years with an older man and why I kept it private for so long.

Success is the only avenue I know. I know that in whatever goal I have, I will accomplish it and I will succeed in it. I don't second-guess my intuition. I always know that things happen for a reason and maybe not in the way that I want them to.

The 20's Chronicles will help you on your journey to success. If you are in your twenties, you will learn and develop a lot while reading this book. The 20's Chronicles' path begins for you now!

1
Family

20 & Negative Family Members

They say family is everything, but is it really?
    The word *family* is very interesting. It should bee people sticking together, but why is there always so much drama within a family? Why do we continually argue and then only get together at someone's funeral? Why do we compete with one another, trying to make our household look better than the other? It's simply wack!
    My story: I have a huge family from both sides of my parents, and I don't talk to the majority of them. Yes, we are all busy, but there are just too many attitudes and too much negativity. I only talk to a selective few, but why? I believe in loving people from a distance. I'm doing my own thing. Is that selfish of me? Maybe! Who knows? But jealousy is thick and blood is thick. Why must it bee that way?
    Can you truly bee around people who are negative all the time and always have something to say and talk about you among others? Is it worth it? Is family really important? Yes, it is! You wouldn't bee who you are today if it weren't for family.

The 20's Chronicles

20 & Loving from a Distance

Now this chapter is not about long distance relationships as it may appear from the above heading. This is about simply loving people from a distance.

People come and go in our lives; it's just the rule of life. Sometimes it's not even purposely. Sometimes it's just people grow apart from each other. Now I sit back and reflect on all the people who have come in and out of my life. I'm not a perfect friend, but I know I'm a loyal and positive friend. I've made mistakes, I hurt some people, but as I grow I know who has value to my life. Evaluating the five people you talk to daily will help you learn who has value in *your* life.

My best friend Chris and I made a list of the five people we talk to daily. We made a pros and cons list, and with this list we realized who has value and who doesn't. Now the question is how do you let go of those people who have no value? Honestly, I couldn't tell you, just know as you mature, people of no value will not bee at your level anymore, and they will eventually leave your life.

20 & Don't Become Who Hurt You

"Don't Become Who Hurt You." I'm about to tell you about society and how it affects us growing up.

Here's a painful truth: in the black community, there are a lot of deadbeat dads, which leaves single mothers to raise us. Then as we get older, we become rebels, have hatred toward our fathers, are taught to bee independent, don't know how to express ourselves to men, think every man is going to leave us, turn out gay, and just let "daddy issues" affect our future as adults. I know it sounds harsh, but get use to my language in this book. I'm blunt!

Why do you have to bee another statistic of this? Why do you have to allow a person to dictate how your future will bee as an adult? Being bitter and having hatred to your father, your mother or other family members will cause you to bee lonely and hold a grudge for the rest of your life. I remember in one of my classes we had to get up and tell a personal story, and the majority of the people were talking about how their fathers weren't in their lives. It is so important that we avoid allowing these types of issues to affect our present life because we will then pass that mindset down to our kids and other people.

My story: I was a typical statistic, but I changed all of that when I moved away from Detroit and really saw that **forgiveness is key** for me to move on and grow as an adult. I love both my parents equally. I don't take sides anymore. I know that they both tried as hard as they could to give me a great life. I lived with my mother the majority of my life after my parents divorced, and it did teach me about being independent. It also taught me about complications with men, but as I get older, I'm past that. I'm a hopeless romantic and don't believe all men are the same anymore.

My advice to young parents reading this is to try to bee in your child's life the best way you can bee. I know you may have baby mama issues and the mother is making you to bee a deadbeat, but honestly try your best. To those baby mothers out there, try your best to co-parent and don't have a guy's kid just to trap him and make him love you. It doesn't work that way all the time. To those young girls who think single-parent homes are bad and wish you had both parents, sometimes two-parent homes are even worse, so quit comparing your home to others' homes.

20 & Family Beef

Realistically, no household is perfect. You can have both parents, have money and still bee a dysfunctional family. So, STOP comparing your families to others' families because we

The 20's Chronicles

all go through stuff.

Here's a definition of "family": a basic social unit consisting of parents and their children, considered as a group, whether dwelling together or not. This definition does *not* say that families are perfect, have to bee blood, argue or bee jealous of one another. As human beings, we are all going to argue, but the limits of arguing shouldn't lead to beefing or not ever talking to each other.

My story: Growing up, I had a lot of family issues, which were out of my control. I literally had to choose sides and loyalty, which is what most families do. I have a huge family on both the paternal and maternal sides, and I'm not close with either side. I wish I had a relationship with certain family members, but life doesn't work that way. You are naturally going to clash with people, and things won't always work out. However, I know if I were to start a family, I would try my best to make sure there is no beef.

Some things are out of your control, and everyone won't get along, but we must bee more supportive with each other. One of the main things that I do regret is not having a relationship with my brothers and sister. It's definitely something that truly affects me now as an adult. I love my older brother Anthony a lot because he was the only one I truly saw. I definitely wished that I had a closer relationship with my youngest brother Joshua and older sister Megan. I love them dearly and wish them nothing but the best. With me moving away as an adult, I definitely am unable to see them as much as I would like. But if you guys are reading this, just know that I truly love you and appreciate you.

Also to my dad's side of the family, if you are reading this, I wish things didn't go the way they did, but everything truly happens for a reason. Just know that I do love you guys and wish you guys nothing but the best. My grandma Sweetie really tried her best to build a relationship with her grandchildren as we got older, and I never understood why. Why now? After her passing away, and as a woman, I truly respect her for that, and I know that she is smiling upon us all. To my mother's side of the family, if you are reading this, I love you guys dearly as well. I wouldn't bee the woman I am today if it weren't for you all. I also would like to shout out to the Reaves family, my auntie's husband's family. I admire you guys' bond with each other; I think it's so beautiful. Grandma Brenda is watching over you guys and smiling.

20 & Your Upbringing Doesn't Determine Your Future

Most of the time, people blame their past when not fully pursuing their dreams or their potential. What I mean by this is that we blame our parents, being from the hood, and not having money in regards to us not succeeding and not getting out of those tough situations.

People make excuses every day when wanting to pursue their dreams. The most common excuse is not having enough money. Most successful people struggled and didn't have anything. So why are you constantly making excuses?

My story: I didn't struggle as much as my family did because my mom always made sure I had everything growing up. Yes, I got everything I wanted as a child, but I always wanted more and saw more for myself as an adult. I want to live a comfortable life where I could travel whenever I wanted to, get up and go and spend however much money I wanted without looking at a price tag, and I knew I would. If that makes me Hollywood, so bee it.

I remember when I first started college; my mom was unemployed and I didn't know how I was going to make it in California. But with faith and God, we made it work. I could've made an excuse about it and not succeed. I also could've been wild in California, but I used my resources and killed it out here.

"I won't let my past destroy my future. I will always

The 20's Chronicles

keep progressing, and you should, too. Start today and not tomorrow."

Busyy Bee Family Quotes!

"You are who you hang around."

"Forgiveness is key."

"Your upbringing doesn't determine your future."

"I won't let my past destroy my future. I will always keep progressing, and you should, too. Start today and not tomorrow."

Busyy Bee Work

⇒ If you've been hurt by a family member or a loved one, write down how you feel about that person, and when you are truly ready, meet with them and simply express how you feel.
⇒ Send cards to your loved ones just because.
⇒ Send a text saying, "I love you" either weekly, monthly or daily.
⇒ Forgive who has hurt you. You can't live a happy life with grudges.

Reflection

After reading this section about family, I've realized how much I have grown as a woman. When I was a teenager, I was bitter about everything and everyone. I held a lot of grudges with a lot of family members. There were a few moments that I remember and want to share with you all.

I remember when I insulted my dad the day of prom. I was so mad and bitter about him not having a relationship with his children and especially with me as I would've liked. I didn't like that he was always with women and not his kids. I didn't like how he just left me and my mom for another woman. It always affected me in high school. I always was in the middle between him and my mother. It was something that I didn't like. I didn't like that my mom didn't want me to bee cool with him because of their divorce. I just wished everyone got along. Although I'm sassy, I'm genuinely a nice girl and like peace. Going back to my prom day, I definitely disrespected him as a man. I can't remember exactly what I said, but everyone said I was wrong, and I could tell it hurt his feelings. I was so mad at myself because I had ruined our relationship until after I left for college. Eventually, I apologized, and he forgave me, and now that's my hommie. I love him, and I realized that I had to bee the bigger person for a brighter future in my life. I had to forgive him and my mother. I think we always view our parents as heroes when we are little and get disappointed at their actions as an adult. In our heads we are like "You are not the person that I thought you were."

What truly inspired me to finish this book was in the summer of 2015. It was all because of family. I had found out so much about my childhood that summer that I just had a mental breakdown. I was literally crying to my friend Shaneka, my aunt Renee and godmother Monike almost every day about my relationship with my parents, especially my mother. I was shocked that I let myself go like that. I was extremely depressed. I had got laid off at WB, I was keeping up with red carpet events and interviews, I had ended an on-and-off relationship, and I had moved by myself. I had just graduated college. It was hard. I felt so alone. I didn't want to add these stories in my book because I would've cried writing everything. But out of it all, I really valued family after these situations. I had to forgive and bee at peace with myself—not them, but myself.

My other regret came when I stopped having a relationship with my aunt Tiffany and step-grandmother Jackie. We would literally bee at her house every day. I couldn't believe as a family we let petty things ruin something so great. We let the incident of my dance crew, which I will talk about later in this book, affect our relationship. We let outsiders and other people's opinions demolish our relationship. Through these experiences, I learned that family is important and that we need to connect more frequently. It's not right to come together only *after* someone is dead.

Another relationship that really hurt me was the relationship I had with my cousin who's a model and actress in the industry that I won't name because she may sue me (Giggles). We used to be extremely close. There had been beef for many years with my dad's family and my mom. Since she was a family member on my dad's side, it was always ups and downs with our relationship. That's why I always tell people it's so important that your family and friends get along with your partner. We fell out over a conversation she had with my mom and her actions while in LA toward me at an event. There were many cases of us falling out. I always loved her and looked up to her because I felt like she made it out of Detroit just like me and killed it. Now the times that I have seen her, she doesn't speak. I never wanted our relationship to bee that way. But I've realized that some people just don't forgive, but as long as you do, your life will bee at peace.

Everything happens for a reason, and I'm in a much better space in my life. Reading these blogs a year since writing them, I believe I am truly at peace.

2
Friendships

20 & You Are Who You Hang Around

"You are who you hang around" is one of the many quotes I definitely have always believed in. Some people don't realize how much value and impact others have in their lives. You have to bee around people who are better than you or at least who are accomplishing the same ideas or goals as you.

I always evaluate the people who are in my life and what their purpose is in my life. Do they make me happy, are they go-getters, are they career driven like myself? Of course every friend is different, but the friends you have in your life must bring some type of happiness into your life and must help you grow as a person.

My story: I had a dance crew called Adamasity back in Michigan when I was 14. It was my aunt Tiffany, my god sister Dede and a few other girls I won't name. We were known for being stuck up, and most people in the city didn't like us. I was young and didn't know how much value these girls had in my life and how I was criticized for just being around them. People didn't like us for several different reasons. See the dance world in Detroit is very small.

The 20's Chronicles

Everyone in some way has danced with each other, met each other or had beef with each other. I was the baby out the group, and I was also very loyal. So I always felt like if you messed with one of them, you mess with me, too. I didn't want to bee known as being stuck up or not liked by many people. So when business went wrong, and money came up missing, people had to go. We had arguments and fights about petty things outside of what we were most passionate about. Looking back, I realize we argued over a petty $100. Because of this fiasco, during my senior year of high school, I decided to not bee friends with anybody but my mother. I had to cut out and evaluate the people in my life. Those girls did make me stronger, but I value friendship way more now.

I am quick to cut people out of my life because I'm on a journey to success, and I know that everyone has an expiration date. I also know that I have an expiration date in others' lives, and I'm okay with that.

20 & Should I Not Like a Person Because My BFF Doesn't?

Loyalty or being dramatic? I remember in middle school when girls would not like other girls because their BFF didn't. These situations are always super tough because of loyalty.

Does this mean you can't bee cool with someone your BFF doesn't like? I personally feel you don't have to not like the person, but you shouldn't converse with them. If you are in an environment where you see someone your friend doesn't like, don't bee rude, do speak, but don't bee having conversations. Also each situation is different because say for instance your friend has two friends, you and another person, and you both just don't like each other. She is loyal to both of you guys not just you.

My story: One of my old best friends was close with me and another girl, and the girl did not like me. The feeling was mutual. I'll call my best friend Krissy and her friend Catherina.

I thought the girl was not the type of person I would hang around. She was super Hollywood and would bee fake one day and cool the next. I didn't force my friend to stop talking to the girl because that was still her friend. I'm not childish like that. I also don't let a person have that much power over my life. One night Catherina invited us to her ex-boyfriend's party at his studio. We arrived before Catherina and sat in the kitchen talking. Catherina walked in, angry.

"Why the fuck are y'all in here?" she asked.

I didn't say anything, but I didn't need to. My face always had something to say.

Krissy got mad at me and said, "Bianca, why the fuck you give her that look?"

"Because she's super rude," I replied.

Unfortunately, that day out of all days, I decided to not drive. After that situation, my friendship with Krissy went downhill. Krissy decided to take Catherina's side, and that was completely fine. In the long run, I was right about that person. Most of the time my gut feeling about people is always right and I never second guess that. Should my old best friend have taken sides? No, I feel like she should've just told both of us to just chill out.

What I want you all to take from this situation is that you have different friends for different things. You have a going out friend, you have a friend you can tell all your secrets to, you have a relationship friend and just an acquaintance. Really establish what friend is for what.

20 & Respect Each Other

Are you the jealous type or the supporting type?

As women we need to start helping and promoting one another instead of bashing and trying to bee better than the next. There is room for everybody to make it and make money. Why hate when you can encourage each other?

I noticed that there is a lot of female empowerment; however, there is still jealousy within supporting each other. Social media has had a few of us wanting plastic surgery, wanting a bigger booty, flaunting how much makeup we have, etc. Why do we need to do all of that? For what?

My story: I noticed that now there are a lot of hosts and a lot of women reaching out to me. I always respond and encourage young girls to start their own show and work hard. The reason for that is at the end of the day no one can bee me. I am Bianca Bee; no one can duplicate what I do, so I don't feel threatened. This is the main thing I teach in my Busyy Bee Bootcamp. I don't want you to bee me. I want you to bee you and bee confident in your brand.

So stop hating and support!

20 & Why You Should Support Other Women

Why are you hating?

Our generation is filled with more women entrepreneurs. Every day more and more women are starting their own businesses. As more women are starting their own businesses, other women are either hating or not supporting, and I wonder why?

Why can't we let the next woman succeed? Oftentimes, the other women aren't even in our field of work, so who are we competing against?

My story: I am a person who loves having a mentor or someone who has had a lot of experience in the industry or just in life. I think having a few women mentors is extremely important because you can gain a lot from them. My fellow women mentors are Monica J., Monica M. and my godmother Monike W. My "M" girls! I also have shadowed a few women hosts because I believe that they could teach me more. I always want to learn from other hosts and get their feedback on my work so I can get better.

Don't bee afraid to shadow other women or write other women congratulating them. Give credit where credit is due.

Stop the jealousy!

20 & 5 Things Successful People Do Daily

Everyone has their own meaning to success, but what I do know is there are a few traits you must have to bee a successful person.

Here are five things I want you to inspire to do:

Work Ethic: This is something that can't bee given to you or even taught. Work ethic is being a consistent hard worker and having diligence.

Balance: You must learn to balance everything in your life, and time management is key! You must know how to bee a boss, a spouse, a friend, a parent, and last but not least a lover of self.

Believe: Know that you will bee successful no matter what. You must also believe in others. Bosses and leaders support each other.

Failure: You must learn that you will fail. Everything in life will bee trial and error, and you must grow from those experiences.

Health: You must take care of yourself from your physical appearance to inner self.

Keep pushing forward daily, and don't give up! Some of my daily dos that help me stay focused are:

⇒ I love reading daily, especially with iBooks and articles online.

The 20's Chronicles

⇒ I write daily because it keeps me sane and motivated.
⇒ I love social media, so I'm always networking.
⇒ Having group chats with friends from out of state is always fun, and it keeps me sane.
⇒ I work out every week.

Busyy Bee Friendship Quotes

"I am quick to cut people out of my life because I'm on a journey to success, and I know that everyone has an expiration date. I also know that I have an expiration date in others' lives, and I'm okay with that."

"Why hate when you can encourage each other?"

"Keep pushing forward daily, and don't give up!"

Busyy Bee Work

⇒ Evaluate the top five people outside of your family whom you talk to weekly and do a pros and cons list of each person (bee honest with yourself), and evaluate if these people bring joy, positivity, and happiness in your life.
⇒ Practice your five daily successful goals that I mentioned in the **20 & 5 Things Successful People Do Daily**.
⇒ Tell a young woman or man congrats on their success.

Bianca Bee

Reflection

As I reread this chapter, I can tell how much I value supporting others and friendships. In my Busyy Bee Bootcamp, I always have the girls in the camp share a personal story they wouldn't share with the world. After we do this exercise, we all shed tears because you don't realize how similar you are to people. You can bee in the room with a stranger and have gone through the same things in life. So treat all people with respect and know that everyone has a story. And to my Adamasity girls, I love you all. You taught me a lot about sisterhood and business. I am glad that we are all mature now to follow and support each other. To my old best friend, I will always love you like I told you at our mutual friend's house. Your friendship taught me a lot about life.

3
Internships & the Entertainment Business

20 & Is College for You?

College isn't for everybody, and that's okay! Some of the most successful people didn't even go to college until years later. Now, I'm not saying don't go to college because I recommend it to the girls I mentor, but really go for something you love. Don't just go because your parents forced you to, don't just go to party, and don't just go because the army pays for it. Go because you want to go, and it truly makes you happy.

Now I went to school for filmmaking, and I have seen people come and go because they simply can't handle it or can't afford it. A lot of people who are pursuing the entertainment industry think when they move to Los Angeles, they will get a job or bee famous like that, but really all of that is super FALSE! What you see on TV is not real life.

So my advice to you is that if you're debating on going to college and trying to figure out if it's really right for you, just simply go with your gut feeling. Don't rush it, college will always bee there! If you need to take some time off, take some time off. Do it for you, not for anybody else! If you can't afford it, get a job and stack your money so you can afford it.

20 & Internships

The Internship Game! Now, everyone always asks me how I got my internship at The Oprah Winfrey Network, TMZ and so on. The response I always say is "I simply submitted online." Internships are and aren't really hard to find. Most companies are always looking for extra "free help," and big companies are always looking for "paid help." I'm going to share with you the game of internships and how to get one.

My resume consists of The Oprah Winfrey Network, After Dark Films, Paramount Pictures, Dark Child Record Company and many more. You, too, can have companies like these on your resume. Consider the following steps in finding internships and applying for one:

1. First, think of the company you always wanted to work for. Then simply say, "I'm going to bee there someday." Sounds corny, but trust me it helps.
2. Second, research internships in your field by going online and talking to your teachers and people in the career services office at your college.
3. Third, work on your resume. Revise your resume a lot before submitting, and get others' opinions. Your resume is crucial, and it's important to be accurate in everything you write on it. For my Oprah submission, my cell number was wrong, and luckily my email was on the resume because I would've missed out on the perfect opportunity. So reviewing every part of your resume is important.

The 20's Chronicles

Now, when you get the call to come in for your dream internship, always use proper business etiquette. When you arrive at your internship, always have your resume in a folder. I always bring my reference sheet just in case and also some people suggest a thank you card. When you are there, bee yourself. A lot of people go into jobs trying too hard. I always go in as if whether I get it or I don't, I won't stop." I also never get my hopes up or tell many people about the internship process because when too many people know, they constantly ask, "Did you get it?"

When you get the internship, always observe. Don't bee so loud or always wanting to meet the top head executives. By observing and researching every aspect of the company, you will potentially get a permanent position at that job. A lot of interns always seek attention. The crazy thing about me is I like attention, but in a work environment I don't. I just sit back, stay quiet and observe.

Biggest suggestion I can give: never tell your personal life in a work environment.

Now RESEARCH, KICK ASS & DO YOUR BEST!

20 & Accepting the Word "No"

Are you tired of hearing the word "NO" when it comes to your career? You feel talented, you feel strong about your work, but you constantly get a NO from your dream job or other people saying your work isn't perfect. **Never let the word "NO" discourage you and make you degrade yourself as a person.**

The word "NO" doesn't mean your work is horrible; it just means that certain job was not meant for you at that particular time. **I always say things happen for a reason, and you should never second-guess yourself.** It's hard to train yourself to have this mindset, but you *can* do it!

Bianca Bee

My story: In September 2013, I applied for a particular internship; I was extremely upset when I found out I didn't get it. It was one of my dream companies to work for. I eventually quit my regular job and put all my focus in my show, and four months later, I got the internship for Oprah. Think about it. If I didn't quit my regular job, I probably would not have been able to balance the two or may have never applied on the free day that I had off. **I believe everything happens for a reason. The advice I can share is that if you are unhappy in a work environment and debating if you should leave or not, always go with your gut feeling.**

Never get upset at "NO" because you may go on a different path in life and something better may come.

20 & The LA Life

When I move to LA, I'm going to bee famous. I'm going to make so much money.

My friends back home think I'm a star, but I'm staying on the couch with a friend. They think I'm in movies, but I'm in a college short film. They think I'm driving a Benz, but I saw it on Rodeo Drive and took a picture by it. The persona of LA is crazy.

LA is one of those cities you have to bee careful not to get caught up in. I've been in LA for over four years now, and it definitely is not what I thought it would bee. LA is one of the most challenging cities; it will open your mind to a lot of things. There are tons of people who are doing the same thing as you, and sometimes it's challenging to stay motivated all the time.

My story: When people would ask me how I liked LA, I would say I loved it. I wouldn't bee here if I didn't love it; however, it does have some flaws to it. I remember when I

The 20's Chronicles

wanted to move to LA just for the Hollywood lifestyle like *The Hills* growing up. Television made Hollywood look so beautiful and lavish. When seventeen hit, and I moved here, I got a quick reality check. I realized you are not going to get famous by living here. Most celebrities are broke; the Internet portrays it to bee better than what it is, but I'm here to tell you that you will encounter some bumpy roads.

Now what I love about this city is the go-getter mentality. Everybody hustles to make it out here. It's always grind mode in a positive way. Everybody does something here, and I love it. I do recommend if you want to bee in the entertainment industry to move here, but bee prepared to struggle a little bit. This city isn't for everybody. I've seen a lot of people come and go.

Below, check out my pros and cons list of LA:

Pros:
- ⇒ Go-getter mentality
- ⇒ Real money out here
- ⇒ Career driven people
- ⇒ Importance of fitness & health here (You will lose weight.)
- ⇒ See wealthy people everyday

Cons:
- ⇒ You don't see celebrities in Hollywood; most of them stay in the valley!
- ⇒ Watch your back, every man and woman for themselves.
- ⇒ Relationships and dating out here suck.
- ⇒ You will not get famous here as soon as you get here.
- ⇒ You will hear "no" a lot.

Bianca Bee

20 & Making the Best Out of Every Situation

We often complain about why this or that didn't happen. Often beat ourselves up when things don't go our way. We want to bee in control of the smallest things, but when we aren't, we often get frustrated and mad. However, you should never question your life because everything happens for a reason.

There are no coincidences or accidents when it comes to life. Once again everything happens for a reason and you should make the best out of every situation. Quit complaining that you don't have the money or the resources to do what you truly love. All that does is bring less money in your life and leave you exactly where you were yesterday.

My story: I often would complain about not having money to do such and such. Or just make excuses for the small things that I couldn't control. I didn't have money for college in the beginning, but I made the best out of my situation and through the grace of God and my parents, I was able to get my degree. I also made the best out of my situation by using my resources and starting my own show. My school had everything: the equipment, the sound stage and I decided why not use these resources and go for it? I created something that was never done before, and that came with a lot of haters and a lot yip yapping people.

Notice the things you say and do daily. Those daily things take a toll over your life. You attract all the negativity that comes your way. Make the best out of every situation and every person that enters your life. Never second-guess the universe or God, whichever you believe in.

20 & Figuring Out What to Do After Graduation

The number one question asked after graduation is *What's next?* I had the same question and hit a bumpy road before

The 20's Chronicles

and after I graduated.

The story: After school, I had a job offer that I thought was major, but was a quick reality check for me. I wasn't making any type of income at my summer job. It was the most miserable job ever. Surprisingly it was on a studio lot; however, I still wasn't happy. I had felt like I was settling for a position when I knew that it wasn't somewhere I wanted to bee.

The thing after graduation that hit me the most was family problems. I had so many family issues after college that I went into depression. I wasn't happy at all. I was living paycheck to paycheck, and then I felt like my career had slowed down. I wasn't doing any press events, and although I was shooting my show, I also had found out that the studio I was shooting at was closing down in Fall 2015, and I was just like *what the hell am I going to do?* I was losing out on a lot of money. I felt like everything was crashing down around me.

Trying to figure out what do next is always so challenging and can bee stressful. The real world hits after college. You have to start paying bills, then when you get a regular job, you eventually may lose focus on what you actually got your degree in. After that bumpy road during the summer, I created a list of things I wanted to do.

Here is a list I created that has worked for me:

⇒ Take a vacation. You have to just simply take a few days off and rest! I had decided to go to New York with my best friend Chris, and it honestly was a trip well needed.

⇒ Create a 10-year plan. Create a plan for the next 10 years of things you want to accomplish in your life. I know it is far ahead, but having this plan can really change your life. I personally love vision boards. They work!

⇒ Don't stress. This is a must; we all know realistically (I hate this word) that the most challenging thing is finding a job that is in your career after college. If you planned ahead before you graduate, then great! That is something I did and although I wasn't happy at my job after college, it still dealt with filmmaking.

⇒ Put yourself first. Please understand that you won't make everyone happy in your decisions after college. You must do it for yourself before anybody else.

⇒ Have courage. This is the biggest one! You must take risks and know that things can change, but have a lot of courage within yourself to understand that you will make it!

Start working on this list now.

20 & Remember Why You Started!

Let's talk about the beginning.

Remember when you first decided why you wanted to start your career? Remember the feeling, the passion, and the excitement? But right now you just don't feel it anymore. You are discouraged! Negative people just keep saying do something else.

Well, I'm here to tell you to remember why you started! Remember why it was so important to you. Remember when you couldn't live a day without doing it. Go back to that moment and you will get inspired.

My story: I remember when I first started my show. All my energy was invested into it. Then around four months later, I started slacking because I started a new job. I had to quit that job to get my focus back, and when I did that, I had tons of interviews and press events that whole summer.

Take a moment and think about why you started.

The 20's Chronicles

Busyy Bee Career Quotes

"Never let the word NO discourage you and make you degrade yourself as a person."

"I always say things happen for a reason, and you should never second-guess yourself."

"Never get upset at NO because you may go on a different path in life and something better may come."

"There are no coincidences or accidents when it comes to life."

"Take a moment and think about why you started."

Busyy Bee Work

⇒ Revise your resume and have a few people look at it.
⇒ Find an internship or mentor.
⇒ Start on your list after graduation.

Reflection

After reading this chapter, I've realized how much I've accomplished at a young age. I always think about my future instead of living in the present. When I did my 2014 vision board, I put Oprah on there. A few months later, I was working for her network. It was a dream of mine to work with Oprah. When I was a blogger, I always loved TMZ. I am so grateful for having worked for these companies.

Although I had a difficult time after college, it was a lesson for me to write this book. I realized that you don't have to have it all figured out yet. I think we compare ourselves to people so much that we want things to happen now, now, now. Realistically we have to bee patient. In this chapter, I want you to understand that timing is everything and to not give up on your dreams just because of a few bumps in the road.

4
Branding & Networking

20 & Branding

BRAND! BRAND! BRAND! Are you working on your brand? Trying to figure out the route you want to go with it is not easy, but I can share what I have learned this far.

Branding is definitely the key to any business and anything that involves putting yourself out there. When I started hosting classes, our teacher always asked us what our brand was, and at the time, most of us didn't have an answer. Branding is hard because we make changes every quarter because the media is changing so much, and we have to always bee relatable.

My story: I started my show in July 2013, and my brand has expanded a lot since then. I remember when I walked into the Queen Latifah internship and the HR knew about my show. Also, a few of my crewmembers have gone into internships and people have heard about it, too. People are hearing more about "Bianca Bee" and who she is. I don't look at Bianca Bee as myself; I look at her as a brand. My brand is Beauty, Entertainment & Everything in Between.

To make myself *known*, I often do the following:

Bianca Bee

- ⇒ I would wear purple lipstick everywhere, and that's how people remembered me. Even the celebrities I've interviewed would say, "Oh, you're the girl with the purple lipstick?"
- ⇒ I also always put a "purple heart and a bee" on everything I tweet and post so when people write me they do it, too.
- ⇒ I write "bee" instead of "be" literally all the time.

Those are just a few hints of how people always remember "Bianca Bee."

One of most successful things I do, the use of "bee," has received negative responses, too.

Here's an email from one of the bitter housing ladies at my college:

Not sure if you're aware, but you spell 'be' with an extra e. Just wanted to let you know if you want to keep your emails professional and correctly spelled.

My response:

I spell "be" like that due to me branding my name as Bianca "Bee," and that works for me. There is no need to address me on that. That has gotten me internships with big companies, such as Oprah's Network, Paramount Pictures and more. Thanks for that little tip! They find it very funny and cute! :-)

As Tamar Braxton would say, "Ms. Jana tried it ☺" Now look at me. I have a whole book with me saying "Bee."

The key to branding is staying consistent and always being memorable.

The 20's Chronicles

20 & Invest in Your Brand Now, No Excuses

Want to start your own business or new career path? Well, stop making excuses and go for it! Quit saying you don't have enough money, quit saying you don't have the resources. You do! This is what the Internet is for. **The Internet has free access to everything you need in life.**

Investing in your brand is so important. Yes, you will come out of pocket for everything in the beginning stages; however, if you are consistent, it will pay off. A lot of people say they want to do this and that, but never do it! A lot of people say they don't have money, but you *can* use the resources you have.

My story: I started investing in my brand when I was 19. My show was in the beginning stages of spending a lot of money. Till this day I don't make profit for my show or what I do, but I love it that much that I do everything out of my own pockets. I hustle! It is stressful, but I know it will pay off. I don't need approval that it will. Investing in my brand is key to me now because I'm starting young. When I was in college, I used my resources and created something that had never been done before. Below, I'm going to share to you guys some things you should do for beginning branding.

1. Build a website
2. Create business cards
3. Start and complete business registration paperwork
4. Create a logo
5. Create and maintain social media pages

Those are a few basics must-dos for having a business nowadays. So start your business now!

Bianca Bee

20 & How Do You Know This Is Your Dream Job?

Is this really what you want, or are you just good at it?

A lot of people are really great at something, but what they do is not their passion. How do you know what your dream job is? How do you know if it's right for you?

Oftentimes, our interests on our career changes, especially if you are talented in multiple things. Just like me. For example, I was a trained dancer all my life. I thought I would dance backup for artists, start my own dance school and go on many tours. I didn't think I would go into media, start a blog and start my own show. You couldn't have told me that when I was younger. I also was a rapper when I was fifteen and took music seriously. Although I was great at those things, God had something better in store for me, and I'm doing exactly what I'm supposed to bee doing at this very moment.

Here is a list of things that can encourage you on having your dream job:

- ⇒ Do the job that makes you feel happy and good.
- ⇒ Do the job that doesn't feel like work.
- ⇒ Do the job that positively impacts your self-esteem.
- ⇒ Do the job that you think about doing every day.
- ⇒ Do the job that doesn't feel like you are settling.
- ⇒ Do the job that highlights who you are.
- ⇒ Do the job that doesn't feel like you are working a 9-5.
- ⇒ Do the job that will enable you to teach others.
- ⇒ Do the job that you are passionate about.

Think about these things when picking a career choice.

The 20's Chronicles

20 & Talking about Your Dreams Instead of Doing

You say you want to bee an actor, dancer or singer, but you aren't seeing results. You constantly say I'm going to bee famous. But in order to do all these glamorous things, you must put in the WORK! You are definitely dreaming instead of doing.

One thing I can't stand is someone who has all these big dreams and goals, but steady on social media, steady chilling, steady smoking and drinking instead of putting the work in. Nowadays people want a handout. They want stuff given to them and will do whatever instead of doing the work. ESPECIALLY WOMEN. Being sexy and sleeping around with big names does not mean you are putting in the work.

My story: I've always been ambitious and a "goal" digger. I've always worked hard even if I was spoiled. So many people write me like how you do this, how did you meet such and such, how did you get into hosting? My response is that I worked my butt off, and I put in the work.

So ladies and gents, if you want something, go for it! **Put in the work, put in those long hours, stay healthy, and realize that you will spend your own money until your career takes off.**

20 & Starting a Show

Most common question I get asked by girls is how do you start your own show? They want to know how to go to press events. How to get into hosting. How to meet celebrities. I'm going to spill it right here in this chapter.

My story: Starting this show was not easy for me because many people bailed on me as far as crew because they weren't getting paid and felt like it was a waste of their time. Which is completely understandable. However, people don't understand starting a business or anything is all about trial

Bianca Bee

and error. I wish I could release content and shoot every week; however, that is a challenge because I have to work with what I have and the people I have. I do not make profit for what I do; I spend money, a lot of money. On clothes, makeup, feeding people, storage for my set and gas. It's been a difficult journey; however, it's been the best journey. A lot of people in college thought I lived this glamorous lifestyle based on how I carried myself. But it wasn't even like that. I just used my resources.

I remember my last quarter of college; one of the faculty members didn't really like me shooting my show at the school. He was an evil person not only to me but a lot of people. I worked with him personally on a popular web series we shot at my college called *Pensado's Place*. I knew his personality and knew he was shady. So it didn't surprise me. However, when all the drama happened with my last quarter in college and shooting my show, my feelings were hurt. I cried like crazy to know that people didn't like me or support what I was doing. But did I show my tears to those people at my school? Hell fuck no! I'm still from Detroit, and we know how to hustle and handle our business. One man don't stop a show, baby. With things like this, you don't give up. It's my brand, and it will pay off, and the people who've been riding with me will see checks one day!

I decided to start my show back in June 2013. At 16, I started my blog in Detroit doing written interviews. When I was 17, I moved to LA to pursue college for filmmaking. I decided that I still liked being in front of the camera and not really behind the scenes as much. I talked to my friend Jessica and roommate Keyanah and told them I wanted to do blogging again but as a show on YouTube. We got crew together, I had my friend invest in me getting my production design, and in July 2013, we did our first test shoot.

When starting my show, I didn't know anything about hosting. I didn't realize it was a skill. I just knew I was good at asking questions. As I watched the beginning episodes of my show, I realized I had an accent. I also slurred my words, and certain things I said didn't come out right. This girl Lynn from school told me about a hosting boot camp with Marki Costello. I went to the free seminar and after that went to her boot camp, then eventually got into her school. I trained for about a total of four months and realized how much I had improved.

As I continued on with my show, in February 2014, I received an Instagram message from a publicist named Shaneka (who is now like my big sister) who asked me to do press for Basketball Wives LA premiere. I wasn't that familiar with press events, but I jumped at the opportunity, and after doing the press event, my social media followers increased. People started believing in me more, and events started coming back to back. After doing that press event, more publicists started to reach out to me to cover their events. This is why I have interviewed a lot of celebrities. **I build relationships with people because it's so important in this industry.**

As I am here today, I have evolved in just over a few years. My goal was to get my name out there the first year and that's what I did. Of course it's going to take more time because I don't have a big company behind me as of yet; however, when it comes to business, I will take my time.

Being an entrepreneur is not easy. You have to sacrifice a lot to get to where you need to bee. It's going to bee a lot of long hours, a lot of investments and a lot of hard to work to make it to the top. Some people are meant to bee leaders, and some are meant to bee followers. You pick which route you want to go.

20 & Let Your Work Speak for Itself

Constantly feel like you have to brag about how hard you work? Always feel like you are competing for people to respect you? Well, you need to stop it and let your work speak for itself.

Nowadays people constantly feel like they have to brag about everything they do when it comes to their career. Always feeling like they have to do a lot in order for a big executive to notice them and their work. But you don't have to do all of that.

My story: When I first started my show, I always texted and sent people the link of my show, and I would get so pissed off that people wouldn't share it. I was hurt, always thinking no one truly supported me. Then I eventually stopped and was like my work will speak for itself I don't have to spam people to look at my work. Now, people pay attention to what I do. I don't have to prove a point anymore. If I get the views, I get the views, if I get the likes, I get the likes. **I know my talents, and I know my work ethic, and by doing the work, it will speak for itself.**

Stop trying to prove yourself to other people. You don't need to do all of that. Simply let your work speak for itself.

20 & Why Networking Is Important

Network to Net-Worth! Can your network determine your net-worth? Absolutely! Especially, if you have an online business. However, don't take that to your head, people. Don't think your followers will determine your bank account numbers that quickly.

Networking is extremely important when you want to establish your name as a brand. You either want to go the positive route of putting your name out there or the negative route. For example, a lot of women use sex to put themselves out there. This is *not* a positive route to take. Establishing who you are is the key to networking. **You have to know who you are a little bit to determine what crowd you want to surround yourself with.** I always believe that

The 20's Chronicles

"You are Who You Hang Around." I've been discussing this very thing throughout the book.

My story: I'm naturally a social person when branding Bianca Bee. I always attend events beneficial for my career and not just the club. I'm also a very social person online; I've always been that way. I'm always sharing my social media profiles with others and staying up to date with what's popular. Now, the difference with me is that I don't do things for popularity; I do it for business purposes. You won't see me with a clique, you will most likely see me by myself or plus one. I'm always aware of what I do when out in public. I never want to see someone post something like, "I met Bianca Bee she was…(Negative comment)." If I remember to act in a professional way, this won't happen.

So remember, knowing who you are is extremely important.

Below are some of my networking tips:

⇒ Always have business cards.
⇒ Try to attend events you are invited to.
⇒ Always bee open to meeting new people who are beneficial to your career.
⇒ Surround yourself with go-getters.
⇒ Always ask or share your social media sites when you meet others.
⇒ Always respond to people online as much as possible.
⇒ Follow people as well, don't act Hollywood.
⇒ Always repeat your name again after meeting people for the first time.

20 & Your Attitude

Are people always constantly telling you that you have a bad attitude, but you really don't? Do you always have to prove yourself to people every second of the day? Do people always tell you, you have a chronic-bitch face, but really you are the happiest person in the world?

Trust me, I know this perfectly. Your attitude will honestly make or break your career as you get older. People don't want to work with a bitch, or even work with someone who might look like a bitch. People will judge you even if you are nice. It's messed up, but that is how this world is. People judge you before even knowing you.

My story: People all my life told me they thought I was stuck up before they met me because of my hair and how I carried myself. It used to upset me because how can you think that based off someone's hair or outer appearance? When I was fourteen and in my dance crew, my attitude became "I think I'm the shit" because I was around people who had bad attitudes, and I thought I knew everything. But when you have a bad attitude, people don't like you or want to work with you. When I moved to California, I had to change that real quick because it could ruin my career. I thought people were so rude here, and it used to make me snap. But once I talked to this girl at my school, she really helped me change my perspective on things. As an African American girl with only just a little bit of us in the film program, she let me know how me snapping on people was not cool. Ever since that day, I've changed. I will slip up here and there because I'm not perfect, but my attitude has changed a lot, and I'm super friendly now, a little bit too friendly because I'm truly happy.

A good attitude is always good to have because you never know who knows whom. You want to always bee a good asset to work with. No one is perfect, and people will try to take you there the majority of the time. ***But every action has a reaction. Bee the good action to have a good reaction.***

The 20's Chronicles

20 & What Your Social Media Profile Says about You

Do you constantly get judged based upon your social media? People always think they know you personally but bee super far off on how you really are. However, **little do you know your social media profile says a lot about you.** What you reveal is a symptom of people interfering in your life. So make sure you reveal accurate information about your life. Also make sure you don't share too much.

Major companies constantly view social media profiles, especially on LinkedIn. These companies research you on social media because they want to see how you represent their company outside of work. Yes, it's annoying and super corny; that's why you have to bee super aware of what you say, what you do and what you reveal to the world.

My story: I had an interview for *The Queen Latifah Show* to be an intern and the HR knew exactly what I did outside of the interview. She knew that I had a show, which I usually don't like for companies to know. I didn't think they would research me, but they sure did. I wasn't mad or anything like that; I was simply shocked. Months later after my internship with The Oprah Winfrey Network, my boss found out I was running a show and was very proud of it. That made me happy, but also I realized that these companies definitely research you.

Always bee aware of what you do, especially if you want to bee in the corporate world. It is extremely important to always bee on your best behavior and don't reveal too much about your personal life.

20 & Proving You Are a Pretty Face & a Businesswoman

Are you a young woman who's attractive, yet still on her grind? Constantly battling people just saying you're a pretty girl? Do you get annoyed with men hitting on you in a work environment?

Trust me, you are not the only one.

Most women in the world use their looks for success. We see this a lot in Hollywood. We see pretty faces, but no talent, which is super wack! It makes it difficult for the woman who are good girls constantly working their butts off for their career. **Having your own business is not easy.** You are thrown obstacles like this too often. You have to bee extremely stern, which may come off as bossy or maybe even flirty.

My story: In my first quarter of film school, this female upperclassman told me that I wouldn't make it far by wearing heels and makeup. At the time I was confused, but then I noticed that most of the women in the film department dressed very manly and acted like men on set. I was like wow, we must downgrade how we look about ourselves to bee respected or not to get hit on? I told myself I would forever remain myself and not change because of the statistics of what society sees us as. And as for the girl who told me I wouldn't make it, she has reached out to me a few times trying to bee a part of my show. So I guess I am doing something right.

Ladies, don't worry about being too sexy or attractive in the workplace. You can't control how you were born. However, **you can control your morals and standards on how people should treat you.** It's okay too bee a pretty face and a businesswoman. You can handle it.

20 & Never Beg People to Support You

Are you always getting upset because people aren't sharing or supporting your product? Well stop it! Quit stressing about it. If you are truly confident in your work and what you're selling or giving to the public, you will bee perfectly fine.

The 20's Chronicles

Begging people to support you will leave you frustrated and depressed. Spamming people with links all day will also make you very upset. Trust me, I know all about it, and it took me time to realize this. However, you must get up and grind, and then your work will show.

My story: When I first started my show, I would get super upset that guests I interviewed would not share or even post a simple picture of being on my show. I remember this one girl from my hometown asked me to interview her, and I made sure I did because I love supporting artists. When the show was aired, the girl didn't even repost, retweet or any of that. It made me realize that people are going to do that because some people care only about their rise. I eventually grew some balls and realized that **everybody is not going to support you or believe in you. That is just life.**

So don't worry about the views on YouTube. They will come. I tell myself this every day. **Just stay focused and continue to work hard, and people will gravitate toward you.**

20 & Why You Can't Do Business with Everybody

Trust is already extremely difficult, but even more so in the business world. You can't work with everybody when it comes to opening and creating businesses. People can screw you over, ruin your career and even ruin your future relationships with others. This is why you have to bee extremely cautious.

When it comes to business you can't bee in your feelings or emotions. You have to determine the right choices by using your brain! Just think about group projects in school? They can either go great or absolutely horrible! Especially, when more than one person tries to lead the entire project.

My story: When starting my brand at 19, I had to become a businesswoman. I had to get out of my feelings about a lot of things and simply use my brain. I had to also use my faith and gut feeling on who was right to do business with and who was super shady. I had one meeting with a guy, and he was simply just trying to know too much about my personal life. I had to move forward without doing business with him because I knew his intentions weren't good, and later, I learned my gut feeling was right.

Bee careful, and use your gut feeling and brain when it comes to business, especially in the entertainment business.

20 & Are You Ready for Criticism?

Taking criticism can bee extremely difficult. Some people just can't take it! People view criticism sometimes as people being haters or unsupportive; however, we all need it at times, whether it's good or bad.

Now what does criticism truly mean? It means the judgment of the merits and faults of a literary or artistic work. Some people may view our work as amazing and others as horrible. But why does it matter? It matters because it should make us better.

My story: I absolutely used to hate criticism. I always thought I was right with literally everything until I went to college. College really opened my eyes on how important criticism is. When you are a filmmaker or an artist, all constructive criticism should bee taken as information that will help you become a better artist. Of course, some people hate, but that's okay; it will make you stronger! One of my teachers Mischa will forever bee one of my favorite teachers. One day he sat down and was real with me. He told me, "You are going places, and you need to learn how to separate your personal life and feelings with your brand." He also taught me a lot with producing my show and getting rid of all the wack people in my life. I will forever bee thankful for him because he was sincere and genuine.

The 20's Chronicles

Criticism is what we all need, so don't get disappointed or discouraged about it. Keep moving forward, and think of it as a gaining more knowledge.

Busyy Bee Career Quotes

"The key to branding honestly is staying consistent and always being memorable."

"The Internet has free access to everything you need in life."

"Put in the work, put in those long hours, stay healthy, and realize that you will spend your own money until your career takes off."

"I know my talents, and I know my work ethic, and by doing the work, it will speak for itself."

"So stop trying to prove yourself to other people. You don't need to do all of that. Simply let your work speak for itself."

"Networking is extremely important when you want to establish your name as a brand."

"You have to know who you are a little bit to determine what crowd you want to surround yourself with."

"So a good attitude is always good to have because you never know who knows whom."

"Every action has a reaction."

"Always bee aware of what you do, especially if you want to bee in the corporate world. It is extremely important to always bee on your best behavior and don't reveal too much about your personal life."

Bianca Bee

"You can control your morals and standards on how people should treat you."

"Just stay focused and continue to work hard, and people will gravitate toward you."

"Criticism is what we all need. So don't get disappointed or discouraged about it, keep moving forward, and think of it as a gaining more knowledge."

Busyy Bee Work

⇒ Review networking tips.
⇒ Revise your social media pages.
⇒ Have people critique your work and projects.

Reflection

This is probably one of my favorite chapters in the book because it's just simply real. You have to stick with your brand and take in criticism and haters. Just like the housing lady who said that remark to me about "bee." I will forever remember that because it will forever motivate me to hustle and continue using "bee" instead of "be."

You are going to encounter people just like her and just like the girl who told me my freshman year I wouldn't make it far by wearing makeup and heels. I dress the part of a CEO. Dress how you wanted to bee treated. Take all the criticism you can, even if it makes you sad. It can only make you better—if you choose to let it.

5
Relationships & Self-esteem

20 & Dating

The Dating Game! I know so much about this. I'm not going to lie, I dated a lot when I moved to LA, and I know you are thinking, "She's only in her 20s. How does she know anything?"

Yes, I know how old I am, and I'm a young woman figuring out what I want for a potential boyfriend in the future, and LA is a tough city for that.

My story: I have to admit that most of my dating experiences did not work out because of me, and I know that, and I'm not afraid to admit that. I always rushed it because I just wanted to bee in a relationship so fast without building a friendship first. I don't regret anybody that I have talked to in the past because those situations were learning experiences, and I am cool with most of the guys I have dated, which many people think is weird.

Now, what I have learned from dating in yours 20s is that you shouldn't just talk to people because you are bored, and that is something I am a victim of. I wanted some attention knowing that I was not really interested in them as people, rather than just their looks. Yes, I have a type and I was just dating that type over and over, which clearly was not good for me.

I've only been in two relationships as a title and two *situationships*, which I've always kept private about on social media. My first boyfriend when I moved to California taught me a lot about why being friends first and just having fun are so important. He and I are still close till this day. The only reason we ended was timing and location. My first situationship was with a person much older than me. We were on and off for three years. We ended because of our age difference and cultural differences because he was Lebanese and I was black. He taught me a lot about being a businesswoman, how to manage my money, interracial dating and being more open. My other relationship was with a guy who taught me a lot about music and introduced me to now one of my good friends Shaneka. That was my only blessing out of that relationship. My special situationship was with a guy I have known since the fifth grade. He was honestly the love of my life. Our problems included our lifestyles and long distance.

I noticed that a lot of girls my age settle for young boys who have absolutely nothing going for themselves and just put up with way too much. One thing I can say is that I have standards, and I won't let a male disrespect me in any shape or form because my standards for myself are high. We don't have many role models but these Instagram models and things we see on social media, which is something we need to work on.

I don't judge anyone's relationship, nor do I compare myself with anybody anymore. I am comfortable now with no longer rushing into a relationship and really getting to know someone. I've always been private about whom I date, which will forever bee my personality because that is what works best for me. However, I'm now taking my time. I know that rushing into something or settling is not what I need to do.

The 20's Chronicles

So think about this: are you just settling or do you really love the person you're currently with?

20 & Self Worth

As you get older, your self worth and standards should bee higher. You should never bee in a situation where you are unhappy or dissatisfied. You should bee able to prove your point and have more confidence in not only your work, but also yourself.

Now what is self worth? And more importantly, why might you lack it? Self worth is the sense of one's own value or worth as a person. Most people lack it for many reasons. Here are a few:

⇒ Because of certain relationships you've had in the past
⇒ Because your parents or friends influenced your behavior toward yourself
⇒ Because you always compare yourself to other people
⇒ Because you never think you are good enough

At some point, we have all gone through this. Always questioning are we good enough, especially for our spouse. Some women and men change who they are while being with someone. They just settle for love or lust. **Confidence doesn't come overnight; however, every day you must grow and learn to love yourself more.**

My story: There have been times I've lowered my standards for a male who didn't have anything going for himself. It made me question my worth. Why was I allowing myself to settle? I'm still learning every day, and I'm still super young, but being aware of this now is forming me to become a better me.

At some point today, question your self worth in your relationship, career and inner self. Question if you are truly happy. Are you just settling because you don't want to bee lonely? Are you changing who you are because of others?

20 & Having Standards

Do you feel like you constantly have to deal with the same bullshit when it comes to men and women? You just constantly keep encountering the same type of people. Well, it's probably because you are lowering your standards on what you deserve.

Sometimes we dumb down ourselves and put up with just anything or anybody because they are attractive or simply just fun to hang around. Why do we accept this behavior if we aren't truly happy? Why are we the ones always taking that extra step for someone who doesn't even have goals or who simply tells us we are beautiful on a day to day?

My story: I have always maintained a relationship with guys who never disrespect me. The only thing disrespectful that has occurred to me is a guy simply not responding to my text messages or a guy simply turning around and getting a girlfriend. However, I've never been called out my name, never got into an argument, or put up with drama with a guy. It's because I set a standard for myself. However, I have messed with guys who have had absolutely nothing going for themselves, and I realized I couldn't date or bee with somebody like that.

You are going to make mistakes; however, don't keep making the same mistakes. It all starts with you first. You establish how a person treats you from the beginning. You initiate the level of respect, what you want and don't want in your relationship. You date at the level of your self-esteem. If you aren't respecting yourself, no one else will respect you either.

The 20's Chronicles

As you get older, your priorities and standards in the beginning will set the tone from the get-go of your relationship with a person.

20 & It's Okay to Be a Good Girl

Are there any more good girls out there? Why do the good girls transform to bad girls? Do you think being a bad girl will get you more attention? What triggered the change?

I've noticed that a lot of once good girls moved to the wild side. They changed how they carried themselves and lowered their standards on how they should bee treated. Seeking attention by showing more of their body on social media, talking more nonsense and being more aggressive. What changed?

My story: I personally think social media has changed a lot of women's perspectives on how they should act. We see girls constantly acting the same by showing so much body rather than showing their grades in college. We get more likes by showing our ass rather than showing our new internship. What happened to the morals? I always remain my good girl status, and I post sexy pictures but in an elegant way that's not trashy. I'm not interested in being hood or acting like somebody I'm not. I'm a good girl, and I know that will bee sexier in the long run as I become an adult.

Ladies, it's okay to maintain your status as a good girl. Just because the girl who is showing her ass gets more likes than you or gets hit on more than you doesn't mean you need to change your good girl ways.

20 & We All Come with Baggage

Ever been talking to someone and they were cool in the beginning, and before long, they let out *all* their secrets? You

Bianca Bee

were head over heels but then found out they had a lot of internal issues.

At the end of the day, talking to someone new can always bee very difficult, especially if they have a lot of flaws and issues. However, it's only up to you if you want to deal with that or not. Don't listen to others about your relationship because others don't know how you two interact with one another in private.

My story: I think in every situation I have encountered, the guys have had a little baggage. I was dating this guy from Philly, and I had really liked him, but the problem was he had just got over a bad breakup. I knew going into the situation to bee very cautious, very understanding and bee simply a friend and nothing more. I saw him kind of down, and it was my choice to accept all his baggage and everything that he was going through. We gradually stopped talking, and although it hurt, I knew from the beginning what I was getting myself into.

Know what you are getting yourself into from the beginning. Communication is key. Communicate what you want so there is no confusion. If you want a relationship and the person you begin dating doesn't, don't get mad about it because you knew that from the beginning. It was your choice to either stay or go.

20 & Why You Shouldn't Say All Men Are the Same

Oftentimes, I hear girls say, "All guys are the same. They are all assholes; they all just want a trophy girl. They don't want an independent girl. Blah blah blah!" Even I've said it. However, it sounds really bitter. Ladies, sorry to tell you, but all men are not the same. Yes, as a species, we all have similarities; however, we are all very different.

Every guy is not an asshole. Every guy is also not a cheater. **Unfortunately, you have to go through a lot of**

assholes to find that one person. From each person you date, you must learn something from the experience. Don't go repeating the same action and allowing the same type of person into your life. If they don't make you happy, simply leave! And don't go back—to that person or another like them.

My story: I grew up thinking all men were the same until I got older and really started dating. Like I said before, there are many similarities in guys, but they are all different. Just like women are all different. Guys can bee one way with you and another way with another woman. Every situation is different. You must learn that relationships may end and that's okay. As long as you learn from each person and don't go repeating your same habits in the next one, you'll be fine.

So ladies, quit being bitter. You will find that person you want and deserve. Don't rush it.

20 & Stop Trying to Force People to Change

What's wrong with a person being who they are?

You can't enter a relationship or friendship trying to change someone. **You cannot change a grown person.** I've been saying this since I was a teenager. Although we strive for others to view our perspectives on life, most people will have their own perspectives, and that is okay.

Of course you should help a person grow, but don't change them. Don't make them dumb down or change who they truly are.

My story: There's this guy from Michigan whom I truly felt like was the love of my life. Yes, I've dated a lot, but this guy has always been special to me. I've known him since fifth grade, and no matter what, he always comes in and out of my life. My love for him will always bee big. Why can't we bee together? Because we come from two different lifestyles. He's from the streets and I'm a good girl. The distance has always been hard for us, too, since I've moved to California. If I were still in Michigan, we would probably bee engaged by now. However, I kept trying to change this person. I wanted him to bee a certain way, treat me a certain way, and he just couldn't do it. I was forcing this person to bee someone he wasn't. I don't have the power to change anyone. I either accept them for who they are or leave them alone.

This situation with Mr. Michigan taught me a lot about myself as a woman. It taught me that you can't wait for people to love you the way you want them to. People grow at their own pace, and since he wasn't ready to commit to me, I couldn't change his decision on that. You can't make someone bee with you or love you the way you want. And as adults, especially women, we always say, "He'll come around. He'll see the good in me." Yeah, he will but at his own timing not yours.

20 & Why Do We Always Go Back to That "One"?

We all have that one person whom we just can't get enough of. You argue, you stop talking for a while and then you are right back to being in love. Why do we constantly go back though? Why can we not get enough of each other? Why was this situation different from any other?

Are you in love, or is it just lust? Are you settling, or are you trying to work things out? Is this person the one, or are you simply just lonely? These are questions only you can answer. It's difficult, but when do you draw the line?

My story: Like I mentioned before, I have that one person who constantly comes in and out of my life. We got mad love for each other, and I don't understand why he has a revolving door to my life. I never really question things in life, but that situation. However, I know everything happens for a reason, and I never question God and His reasons.

Don't let your relationship become routine. If you aren't

happy with a person coming in and out of your life, close that chapter with that person. Quit allowing people to have access to you when *they* want to.

20 & Why I'm Glad I Didn't Have a Serious Relationship During College

Why am I'm glad I put my career before a relationship?

Looking back on my college experience, I'm so glad I wasn't in a serious relationship. I know it may sound super weird to my close friends who know how much I love "love!" But I'm glad I didn't get into anything serious.

My story: Of course, I had my boos, my baes here and there, but they all didn't work out for a reason. And I think that reason is God wanted me to stay focused on maintaining my honor roll status and staying career driven. If I would've been in something extremely serious, I would've been distracted, not focused and may even had drama in my life and an extra headache!

I encourage anyone who is entering college to bee single for as long as possible. If something feels right, then go for it, but if someone is all games, continue to focus on you, boo! "Don't let boys come in between your coins." Love this quote by Taraji P. Henson! It's super true!

20 & People Come in Your Life for a Reason

As I enter into this last section in my book, I want you guys to understand that life will give you many tests. Either you past, get an average grade or fail. You have to understand that you don't go through heartaches, tears, and happiness for nothing. Everything happens for a reason, and everyone comes in your life for a reason.

I'm a firm believer that everyone comes in your life

Bianca Bee

to teach you something. Whether they break your heart, hurt you, betray you, help you, everyone has a purpose. **You have to adapt the belief that you must learn something from everyone who enters your life.**

You're going to go through many friendships, many relationships and changes of career. You must learn from every one of these moments.

My story: I have had many people come in my life, especially friends and guys. I believe that I've learned something from each of them. I take everything I have learned and try to create a better me. Now being older, I know I'm going to mess up, but at least I learned. I learned from family that you must forgive them and their mistakes. I've learned that friends come and go, and that's okay. I learned from my relationships that building a friendship is key and you set the standards on how a guy treats you from the get-go.

What I want you to take from this book is to not let your past situations affect your present adult decisions. In your 20s you won't have it figured out, and that's okay. You have to learn and develop what your purpose is in life and how you can leave a legacy.

Busyy Bee Relationship & Self- esteem Quotes

"Are you just settling or do you really love this person?"

"Confidence doesn't come overnight; however, every day you must grow and learn to love yourself more."

"You cannot change a grown person."

"I'm a firm believer that everyone comes in your life to teach you something."

The 20's Chronicles

"You have to adapt the belief that you must learn something from everyone who enters your life."

Busy Bee Work

⇒ Write down 10 things you love about yourself.
⇒ Write down what you want in your relationships.
⇒ Accept people for who they are.

Reflection

After rereading this chapter, I see that I have grown so much as a young woman. To see where I was then to where I am now in my love life is crazy. My friend Monica M. always cracks up at me on how much I've grown just from sitting on her couch in 2014 going crazy over a text message until now. I've grown to love me first, and I've truly learned to bee alone. I had to build up my confidence and heal a lot of wounds to get to where I am now.

Ending my three year on-and-off situationship with Godfather was something I had to do to get me right. Although he was a great man, he wasn't for me at that time. Getting rid of Mr. Michigan and being at peace with our friendship is something I had to go through. Sometimes we have to get us right first before we get with anybody. Timing is everything, and you need to bee "whole" first as my pastor would say before being with someone. I also learned to not rush relationships; it takes time building a relationship with someone, and I know that now.

Ladies, love *you* first.

Bianca Bee

My Final Words

Your twenties are all about learning about you, loving you and finding your purpose in life. I started writing *The 20's Chronicles* my last month of being twenty. In the two years since then, I've grown so much. I plan to further develop this book because my perspective on life will definitely change throughout these years.

Although I'm young, I have accomplished so much in my life. I am blessed in so many ways. I hope you've gained a lot while reading this book. I wanted you guys to learn that you can do anything you want to in life. Your past or upbringing doesn't determine your future, only you do. Don't stop hustling or working hard because of the industry or how many Nos you encounter in your life.

I thank my parents for giving me the life they did, and I thank my stepdad Daryl, aunt Renee and grandma Shortie for always being my helping hand. I thank my best friends Chris and Melissa for being so loyal to me. I thank my mentors Monica J., Roger, Monica M., and godmother Monike for always reviewing my work and my resume, helping me through my internships, and more. I thank my whole Bianca Bee Show team: Jessica, Mikey, Maureen, Tabytha, Joel, Eric, Kevon, Keyanah, Kristina, Kenia, Eboni, Donovan, and my social media queen Rochelle. Thank you to DeDe for helping

Bianca Bee

me grow into the young lady I am today and giving me advice throughout my teenage years. Big thanks to my friends Laurin, Kristina, Colby, Jasymn, Kasha, and my bro Cameron. Thank you to my favorite publicists and friends Shaneka, Sabrina, and the new addition to my team Bianca. Thank you to my friends Kim, Garry and Fushia for helping me build a better relationship with God.

Thank you to Carl and Jaz for being the best event planners for The Bianca Bee Foundation. Thank you to Moe my web designer and designer of my book cover. Thank you to Natalie and Monique for giving me the courage to write this book. Thank you to my book editor Shonell for being amazing and helping me grow as a writer. I dedicate this book to my little cousins Marzet, CJ and Maya; I want to give them the best life. Thank you to my family for guiding me to how I want my family to be in the future. Thank you to the men who've guided me to the woman I am today. I thank my Texas boy Godfather and Mr. Michigan for always believing in me. MY EP Family: Gerald, Danny, Helene and Marlene. Last but not least, I thank my Busyy Bees and BeeOriginal girls for always supporting me.